THE DIGITAL CLASSROOM

THE DIGITAL CLASSROOM

SLOANE MONTGOMERY

CONTENTS

1. Introduction — 1
2. Benefits of Digital Classrooms — 5
3. Challenges in Implementing Digital Classrooms — 9
4. Digital Tools and Technologies in the Classroom — 13
5. Pedagogical Approaches for Digital Classrooms — 17
6. Digital Assessment and Feedback — 21
7. Digital Citizenship and Online Safety — 25
8. Future Trends in Digital Education — 29
9. Conclusion — 33

Copyright © 2024 by Sloane Montgomery
All rights reserved. No part of this book may be reproduced in any manner whatsoever without written permission except in the case of brief quotations embodied in critical articles and reviews.
First Printing, 2024

CHAPTER 1

Introduction

The rapid advancement of digital technology has revolutionized numerous industries, and education is no exception. **Digital education** encompasses a wide range of activities from online learning platforms to virtual classrooms and digital resources, reshaping how knowledge is imparted and received. It involves multiple stakeholders, including students, teachers, infrastructure providers, and employers who seek skilled professionals. Each stakeholder has distinct needs and contributions, creating a complex ecosystem that drives the globalization of education and intensifies competition among educational institutions, both locally and internationally.

Stakeholders in Digital Education

1. Students: Students are at the heart of the digital education revolution. They benefit from increased accessibility to resources, flexible learning schedules, and personalized education paths. Digital platforms enable them to learn at their own pace, revisit challenging concepts, and engage with interactive content that enhances understanding.

2. Teachers: For educators, digital tools offer new ways to deliver content, assess student performance, and provide feedback. They can leverage multimedia resources to create engaging lessons and utilize data analytics to tailor instruction to individual student needs.

Professional development opportunities also expand through online courses and collaborative platforms.

3. Infrastructure Providers: These stakeholders include technology companies that provide the tools and platforms necessary for digital education. Their innovations enable seamless communication, efficient administration, and secure data management, ensuring the effective operation of digital classrooms.

4. Employers: Employers play a crucial role by outlining the skills they require from future employees. They influence curriculum development to ensure that educational programs are aligned with industry needs, thereby enhancing employability and economic relevance.

Market Dynamics and Technology Enablement

The intersection of market dynamics and technological advancements creates unique value propositions for each stakeholder. Different educational providers adopt various approaches to emphasize aspects such as quality, efficiency, and effectiveness. These strategies are crucial in highly competitive economies like the United States, where differentiation in educational offerings drives transformation.

This paper aims to analyze the digital education transformation by examining the strategies adopted by educational institutions, the intellectual properties they create, and the impact of these strategies on other institutions. The analysis involves understanding the strategic interactions among numerous educational entities in the United States, focusing on the financial and globalization-driven competition that shapes their objectives.

The Growing Investment in Education

Research indicates that global spending on education is poised to reach $6 trillion by 2017, with nearly 99% of this investment stemming from the private sector. Notably, India represents a significant share of this investment, with its education sector growing at nearly

20% annually. The increase in student numbers has spurred competition among domestic and international private players, challenging established national and regional institutions to innovate and improve their offerings.

This substantial growth is driven largely by new education providers and established institutions adopting innovative models enabled by modern digital and information technologies. The rapid growth of communication and information technologies has been foundational, making digital education not only possible but also viable and pragmatic. As the education sector transitions from the physical to the digital realm, it moves closer to the student, offering greater flexibility and customization. Students now have the autonomy to learn what they want, when they want, creating a more personalized and effective educational experience.

CHAPTER 2

Benefits of Digital Classrooms

The advent of digital classrooms has led to significant advantages over traditional classroom setups. These benefits span various aspects, from reducing physical burdens on students to enhancing their learning experiences and increasing accessibility to education. Let's delve into these advantages in detail.

Reduced Physical Burden

In traditional classrooms, students are often required to carry multiple textbooks and notebooks as per their timetable. This can be quite heavy and cumbersome, especially for younger children, leading to physical strain and discomfort. In contrast, digital classrooms allow students to carry lightweight devices such as tablets. These devices can store a vast number of textbooks and notes, drastically reducing the physical load that students have to bear. This shift not only contributes to the overall health and well-being of the students but also makes their educational experience more comfortable and less stressful.

Enhanced Learning Experience

Digital classrooms provide an enhanced learning experience by integrating interactive and engaging content. Traditional textbooks can sometimes lead to boredom and eyesight discomfort due to prolonged exposure. On the other hand, digital platforms can offer interactive learning materials with dynamic content that can adjust to the student's environment, thus reducing eye strain and making learning more enjoyable.

For instance, using technologies like LiDAR, which measures the distance between objects and adjusts lighting accordingly, students can have a more comfortable visual experience. Additionally, the advent of the Internet of Everything (IoE) has made it possible for students to access vast amounts of information quickly, leading to improved knowledge acquisition and retention. Innovative technologies, such as microencapsulated fragrances, have also been introduced to enhance the learning process by improving memory retention through sensory stimuli.

Increased Access to Education

Digital classrooms have the potential to democratize education by increasing access for students around the globe. Many countries, especially in Africa, have made significant strides in bringing education to more people through the development of digital infrastructure and new educational institutions. For example, the introduction of new universities and schools in Kenya signifies a commitment to expanding educational opportunities.

Despite these efforts, many countries have yet to achieve universal primary education. Digital classrooms offer a viable solution to bridge this gap by making education more accessible to children in remote or underserved areas. This aligns with global goals such as the UN Millennium Development Goals, which aim to achieve universal primary education.

Improved Collaboration and Communication

Technology facilitates improved collaboration and communication among students and educators. Digital classrooms enable seamless sharing of resources, peer interactions, and collaborative learning, regardless of geographical location. Projects like the Jamie Project demonstrate how digital platforms can create vast databases of ideas and solutions, enhancing group learning and idea exchange. The flow of information is crucial for effective decision-making, and digital tools have awakened a new era of collaboration. Computer literacy has become an essential skill, allowing students to collaborate on projects, co-author documents, and participate in global learning communities. This collaborative approach not only enriches the educational experience but also prepares students for a connected, digital world.

CHAPTER 3

Challenges in Implementing Digital Classrooms

Implementing digital classrooms is not without its challenges. These challenges can be broadly categorized into six areas: professional development, choosing and using operational digital tools, planning fully integrated in-class scenarios, feedback-based assessment, overall assessment, and closing the learning feedback loop. Each of these areas presents unique obstacles that must be addressed to ensure successful integration of digital education.

Professional Development

One of the primary challenges is ensuring that educators are adequately trained to use digital tools effectively. Many professors and teachers lack the necessary skills to integrate these technologies into their teaching methods. Professional development programs must be designed to help educators gain proficiency not only in accessing and communicating information but also in analyzing and producing multimedia content. As these skills are often second nature to the younger generation, traditional educators need targeted training to bridge the gap and adapt to digital tools.

Infrastructure and Connectivity Issues

A robust infrastructure is essential for the successful implementation of digital classrooms. This includes secure and accessible cloud facilities provided by the National Knowledge Network (NKN) to ensure equitable access, cost-effective operations, and enhanced utilization. High-speed connectivity and reliable cloud services are crucial for facilitating interactive learning, collaboration, and evaluation of learning outcomes. Encouraging the growth and support of regulatory bodies like the Telecom Regulatory Authority of India and the Department of Telecom to ensure Quality of Service (QoS) is key to overcoming connectivity challenges.

Teacher Training and Support

Teachers play a crucial role in the educational process, and their ability to effectively use digital tools is paramount. Engaging teachers with suitable training and support, as well as providing an enjoyable experience with the technologies, can help integrate new teaching and learning methods into the education system. Initiatives such as the Government's Education For All programs in developing countries aim to expand educational reach, but practical support for teachers is essential to make these programs successful.

Privacy and Security Concerns

As educational institutions collect increasing amounts of student data, privacy and security concerns become more significant. Protecting students' personal data requires a shift in thinking towards empowering students to manage and protect their own data. Schools and higher education institutions must maintain appropriate control over IT managers' discretion and set security standards to safeguard student data. Policymakers should address the baseline evidence on the security postures of schools and how they manage this data to prevent breaches and maintain trust in the educational system.

Feedback-Based Assessment

Implementing effective feedback-based assessment methods is another challenge. Digital tools can provide real-time feedback and analytics on student performance, but integrating these insights into the teaching process requires careful planning and execution. Educators must be trained to use these tools to tailor their instruction and provide personalized feedback to students, thereby enhancing the learning experience.

Overall Assessment and Closing the Learning Feedback Loop

Finally, developing comprehensive assessment methods that go beyond traditional testing is crucial. Digital classrooms offer the opportunity to assess students' progress through various means, including interactive activities, multimedia projects, and collaborative assignments. Closing the learning feedback loop involves continuously evaluating and improving the educational process based on feedback from students, educators, and the technology itself. This iterative process ensures that digital classrooms evolve to meet the needs of all stakeholders effectively.

CHAPTER 4

Digital Tools and Technologies in the Classroom

Digital tools and technologies can greatly enhance students' acquisition of technological skills, support innovative learning techniques in STEM education, provide instant assistance to special learning needs, enable 24/7 access to learning resources, and encourage active participation and engagement. These tools support flipped and blended learning styles, stimulate collaboration across multiple locations, and provide immediate feedback. They also help teachers improve productivity and enhance education by connecting students with real-world experiences.

Learning Management Systems (LMS)

Learning Management Systems (LMS) like Moodle are at the heart of e-learning. They provide a platform where students, teachers, and other participants in the educational process can interact through a computerized network. LMSs allow for flexible and efficient teaching models with both synchronous and asynchronous interactions.

Advantages:

- **Accessibility:** Educational resources like texts, videos, and activities can be accessed at any time.
- **Flexibility:** Allows for flexible scheduling and interaction with course coordinators and peers.
- **Resource Management:** Facilitates the management of online tests, forums, and other educational resources.

Disadvantages:

- **Depth of Evaluation:** Some students find that LMSs do not adequately evaluate in-depth understanding.
- **Interaction Challenges:** There may be a lack of interaction among students regarding problem-solving abilities.

LMSs have been used to teach scientific concepts through virtual laboratories and blended learning experiences, enhancing the overall educational process.

Online Collaboration Tools

Online collaboration tools are essential for students who are part of blended learning environments. However, both students and educators often lack the collaborative skills needed to maximize the potential of these tools. Collaborative learning requires a continuous five-step process: commitment to tasks, organizing efforts, streamlining actions, motivating peers, and developing an organized understanding.

Examples:

- **Duke University Energy Initiative:** Offers online lab spaces for collaborative learning.
- **Online Science Library at the University of Waterloo:** Provides resources for scientific collaboration.

Despite their potential, many online tools remain underutilized due to a lack of collaborative skills among users. Educators must be trained to create effective blended learning environments.

Interactive Whiteboards and Projectors

Interactive whiteboards (IWBs) and projectors are transforming traditional classrooms into dynamic learning environments. Initially used for showing video materials and slide shows, digital projectors are now widely used for multimedia presentations, demonstrations, and annotations.

Benefits:

- **Student Engagement:** Keeps students' attention with multimedia content.
- **Interactive Learning:** Allows for interactive lessons with the capability to advance slides and control applications remotely.
- **Cost-Effectiveness:** Digital projectors and IWBs are becoming more affordable and accessible.

While traditional whiteboards and projectors are still in use, IWBs are quickly becoming the new standard in schools. In Europe, the adoption rate of IWBs has significantly increased, with a majority of teachers using them regularly.

Other Digital Tools

Interactive Whiteboards and Projectors: These tools are increasingly becoming standard in modern classrooms. They allow teachers to present multimedia content, demonstrate complex concepts, and interact with students in real-time.

Student Response Systems: Tools like clickers or mobile apps enable instant feedback and active participation during lectures. They help gauge student understanding and adjust the teaching pace accordingly.

Web Technologies: Online platforms and resources provide vast amounts of information and interactive content that can enhance learning. They support research, collaboration, and communication beyond the classroom.

Set-Top Devices and Tablets: These portable devices make it easy for students to access learning materials anywhere and anytime. They support a range of educational apps that cater to different learning styles and needs.

By incorporating these digital tools, classrooms can become more interactive, engaging, and effective in meeting the diverse needs of students.

CHAPTER 5

Pedagogical Approaches for Digital Classrooms

The integration of digital technologies into the classroom has brought about a variety of pedagogical approaches aimed at enhancing the learning experience. These approaches emphasize interactive, student-controlled learning opportunities, thereby transforming the role of teachers and making the educational process more dynamic and engaging.

Blended Learning

Blended learning combines traditional face-to-face teaching with digital tools and resources. One of the main resources used in this model is the Learning Management System (LMS), which serves as a one-stop shop for all educational materials and activities. LMS platforms offer videos, presentations, simulations, assignments, and quizzes, enabling teachers to monitor student progress and make necessary adjustments.

Advantages:

- **Flexibility:** Students can access learning materials at any time and from any location, provided they have an internet connection and a digital device.

- **Resource Optimization:** Teachers can prepare lessons in advance, optimizing their time and resources.
- **Interactive Content:** Students benefit from multimedia content and interactive activities, making the learning process more engaging.

However, the success of blended learning depends on students having access to digital devices and a stable internet connection, which can be a barrier in some regions.

Flipped Classroom

The flipped classroom model reverses the traditional teaching approach by introducing students to new material outside of class, typically through video lectures or online resources like Khan Academy. Class time is then devoted to activities that reinforce and deepen understanding through collaborative and interactive learning.

Advantages:

- **Student-Centered Learning:** Students take responsibility for their own learning, allowing teachers to focus on guiding and facilitating in-class activities.
- **Active Engagement:** Class time is used for problem-solving, discussions, and hands-on activities, enhancing student engagement and understanding.
- **Immediate Support:** Teachers can provide immediate feedback and support during class, addressing any difficulties students encounter.

This model helps students develop critical thinking and problem-solving skills by applying knowledge in a supportive environment.

Personalized Learning

Personalized learning tailors educational experiences to individual student needs, preferences, and learning styles. Digital platforms like the SABIS Digital Platform (SDP) use machine learning and data analytics to create customized learning paths for each student, based on their performance across various subjects.

Advantages:

- **Customized Learning Paths:** Students receive targeted instruction and resources that address their specific needs and learning gaps.
- **Enhanced Engagement:** Personalized learning keeps students motivated and engaged by providing content that is relevant to their interests and abilities.
- **Continuous Improvement:** Ongoing assessment and feedback help students improve their performance and achieve their learning goals.

Schools like Liceo Ingles, part of the SABIS Network, have successfully implemented personalized learning systems, tracking student performance and adjusting instruction accordingly. This approach ensures that each student receives the support they need to succeed.

Computer-Based Instruction (CBI)

Computer-Based Instruction (CBI) provides interactive, student-controlled learning opportunities. It enhances constructivist instruction by allowing students to actively engage with the material through dialogue, collaborative tutoring, cooperative learning, and group work. CBI transforms learning into a cooperative, interactive process, treating the classroom as an application environment where students can create and manipulate information in powerful ways.

Advantages:

- **Interactive Learning:** Students benefit from interactive and engaging learning activities that promote critical thinking and problem-solving skills.
- **Collaborative Opportunities:** CBI encourages collaboration and peer learning, enhancing the educational experience.
- **Teacher Involvement:** Teachers play a crucial role in guiding and facilitating learning, making the process more dynamic and effective.

The integration of computers into the classroom has redefined the role of teachers, highlighting their importance in the educational process and enhancing their ability to deliver effective instruction.

CHAPTER 6

Digital Assessment and Feedback

Digital assessment and feedback are crucial components of the digital classroom, offering numerous benefits such as immediate and actionable feedback, personalized learning paths, and enhanced student engagement. Micro-interaction analytics, online quizzes, automated grading systems, and real-time feedback tools are some of the key elements that contribute to the effectiveness of digital assessment.

Micro-Interaction Analytics

Micro-interaction analytics provide intrinsic motivation by showing progress, offering immediate feedback, grouping students by skill level, encouraging collaboration, and reducing anonymity. By analyzing students' interactions with educational software, educators can gain insights into their learning processes and adjust their teaching strategies accordingly.

Advantages:

- **Immediate Feedback:** Students receive real-time feedback on their performance, allowing them to correct mistakes and improve their understanding.

- **Collaboration:** Grouping students with similar skill levels fosters a collaborative learning environment.
- **Actionable Insights:** Teachers can identify areas where students struggle and provide targeted support.

Online Quizzes and Exams

Online quizzes and exams offer several advantages over traditional paper-and-pencil tests. They are flexible, can be administered over multiple days to reduce academic dishonesty, and can be aligned with other computer-based assessments.

Advantages:

- **Flexibility:** Online assessments can be conducted without time and space constraints, accommodating diverse student needs.
- **Accessibility:** Students with disabilities can receive the same accommodations as with other digital course materials.
- **Efficiency:** Automated grading increases the speed and consistency of feedback, allowing for class-wide adjustments based on results.

Examples:

- **Practice Quizzes:** Allow unlimited attempts and provide explanations for correct answers.
- **Automatically Graded Quizzes:** Serve a summative function by assessing students' understanding of the material.
- **Just-in-Time Quizzing:** Administered immediately after presenting new content to reinforce learning.

Automated Grading Systems

Automated grading systems, such as those used in adaptive learning platforms like Knewton and Smart Sparrow, provide personalized feedback and tailored learning experiences. These systems score answers based on a gold standard and a pre-specified scoring scheme, considering important semantic units in students' responses.

Advantages:

- **Personalized Learning:** Adaptive platforms tailor instruction to individual student needs, allowing for mastery of content at their own pace.
- **Efficiency:** Automated grading reduces the time and effort required for evaluating student work.
- **Consistency:** Provides uniform feedback and reduces subjectivity in grading.

However, automated grading systems may struggle with incoherent responses, which human graders can evaluate more effectively.

Real-Time Feedback Tools

Real-time feedback tools, such as QR codes and geolocation software, enhance the learning experience by providing immediate feedback and identifying material that needs to be revisited. These tools can be embedded into presentations, allowing for interactive and engaging learning activities.

Advantages:

- **Immediate Feedback:** Teachers can identify and address students' misunderstandings in real-time.
- **Engagement:** Interactive features and multimedia resources make learning more engaging.
- **Accessibility:** QR codes and mobile applications provide easy access to digital resources.

Examples:

- **QR Codes:** Used to access model answers, recordings, or quizzes.
- **Geolocation Software:** Tracks students' clicks and provides instant feedback, facilitating m-learning.

By incorporating these digital assessment and feedback tools, educators can create a more dynamic and effective learning environment that meets the diverse needs of students.

CHAPTER 7

Digital Citizenship and Online Safety

Today's students must become well-rounded digital citizens through the integration of digital citizenship into all areas of their curriculum, such as health and character development. This enhancement must occur daily throughout the year to ensure comprehensive coverage of digital safety and citizenship. The digital landscape in which students live and learn is evolving rapidly. Their learning experience extends far beyond traditional textbooks, libraries, and computer labs. Students are connected to digital devices 24/7 and can access vast amounts of information anytime, anywhere. Therefore, being a responsible digital citizen is essential. Special attention must also be paid to students' social-emotional well-being, as both their actions in the digital world and the stress and fatigue caused by it have significant impacts.

Digital citizenship involves participating in online society by understanding the rules, norms, and behaviors appropriate for both technology and community interactions. It includes the safe and healthy use of digital technology for communication, information access, learning, exploration, and creation across devices, media, and platforms. Personal safety, protection, and privacy are crucial topics, but offline behavior is also important to reinforce social norms in the digital space. Digital citizenship encompasses respect, education, literacies, access, and personal protection on various critical topics.

Teaching Responsible Internet Use

Education World's CyberSmart! curriculum offers educators seven standards to teach online etiquette for grade levels 1-12. These standards cover a range of topics from "appropriate technology behavior" to "intellectual property." Each standard is broken down into concepts and lessons, providing detailed information about what students should learn at their age and grade level. This curriculum-based approach is innovative as it integrates the teaching of responsible online behavior into the learning process.

Another program, which offers young students games and videos about cyber safety, helps teachers and students learn about online responsibility. Educators agree that responsible online activity requires explicit educational efforts. Although most teachers include discussions about responsible use in their classrooms, these discussions are often reactive rather than proactive, occurring after problems arise. Older students, in particular, may ignore cyber ethical guidelines, feeling entitled to say whatever they want while remaining anonymous behind their screens. Therefore, teaching responsible internet use from an early age is crucial.

Cyberbullying Prevention

The lack of non-invasive security education tools in children's everyday use is highlighted in the literature. Inspired by the educational guide "Growing Up with Google," which has been successfully implemented in the Romanian education system, efforts are being made to promote digital security competence from the first classes when children start using mobile phones. This guide has been translated and distributed to Romanian parents and teachers.

A mobile application (mApplication) for children's digital security education helps prevent risks like cyberbullying by promoting responsible online behavior. This tool aims to combat misbehaviors such as cyberbullying and manipulation on social networks, ensuring that children are informed and behave responsibly online.

Privacy and Data Protection

Digital education tools and platforms involve processing personal data. Under the European General Data Protection Regulation (GDPR), personal data includes any information relating to an identified or identifiable natural person. Since children's learning is highly personal, learning data can become personal data. GDPR requires stricter handling of children's data, and children under 16 cannot provide valid consent for their profiling.

Digital education tools offer opportunities to enhance the quality and accessibility of learning materials, but they also raise concerns about the use of children's data. Parents worry about their children's data privacy, and schools must adhere to data protection principles. This section provides an overview of the data protection implications for schools using digital education platforms, including privacy threats, applicable privacy standards, and industry compliance.

CHAPTER 8

Future Trends in Digital Education

Technological advancements are deeply influencing the way we think, work, and interact with each other and our environment. As digital transformation accelerates, the education system must adapt to keep pace with these changes. The demand for skilled labor is continuously increasing, requiring a basic knowledge of essential tools for professional life. Educational institutions, both public and private, must strategically use digital platforms to drive improvements and keep up with technological transformations on the horizon.

Virtual Reality and Augmented Reality

Virtual reality (VR) and augmented reality (AR) are revolutionizing the educational landscape. VR immerses users in a fully artificial digital environment, while AR enhances the real world with digital visual elements, sound, and other sensory stimulations. These technologies are still in their early stages, but developers are creating learning programs that use VR and AR to provide immersive and interactive experiences.

Examples:

- **Virtual Field Trips:** Students can take immersive journeys to places like the Great Barrier Reef, exploring underwater environments without leaving the classroom.
- **Interactive Learning:** Students can manipulate 3D objects that appear in their real physical space, enhancing their understanding of complex concepts.

The use of VR and AR in education can save time and money while providing a deeper understanding of the material.

Artificial Intelligence in Education

Artificial intelligence (AI) has the potential to transform education by extending human cognitive and functional capacities. AI can adapt the pace of teaching and learning to the characteristics of each student, providing personalized learning experiences. This technology can enhance the quality of the teaching-learning process and support educators in delivering effective instruction.

Applications:

- **Personalized Learning:** AI systems can adapt to each student's learning style and pace, providing tailored instruction and feedback.
- **Enhanced Teaching:** AI can support teachers in identifying the best strategies for transmitting knowledge, making informed decisions based on data.

AI in education can improve student outcomes by making the learning process more efficient and personalized.

Gamification and Game-Based Learning

Gamification and game-based learning involve using game elements in the learning process to increase student motivation and engagement. These approaches create an interactive learning environment that enhances both affective and cognitive skills.

Examples:

- **Challenges and Quests:** Learning activities can include challenges and quests that motivate students to achieve their goals.
- **Rewards and Competence:** Students receive rewards for completing tasks, fostering a sense of accomplishment and competence.

Gamification promotes a discovery-oriented learning process, encouraging students to follow their intellectual interests and engage deeply with the material.

The Future Classroom

The future classroom will be a dynamic and flexible environment, integrating various digital tools and technologies to enhance the learning experience. Key trends include:

- **Flipped Classrooms:** Combining video lectures watched at home with interactive, hands-on activities in the classroom.
- **Virtual Office Hours:** Using video conferencing tools like Zoom and Adobe Connect for meetings between students and instructors.
- **Blended Learning:** Mixing traditional face-to-face teaching with digital resources and online activities.

As these trends continue to evolve, the education system must remain adaptable and responsive to the rapid pace of technological change, ensuring that students are equipped with the skills and knowledge they need for the future.

CHAPTER 9

Conclusion

The digital transformation in education has profound implications, as evidenced by the increasing adoption of Technology-Enhanced Learning (TEL) across various educational sectors in India and worldwide. The evolving digital classroom fosters an engaging and collaborative environment where students learn not only from instructors but also from their peers, creating a dynamic and interactive learning experience.

Creating engaging content is merely the first step. Effective educational content must be designed for cognitive engagement, personalized, contextually relevant, and aligned with specific learning outcomes. High-quality learning experiences can be ensured through AI-enabled adaptive platforms, spaced repetition tools, simulation platforms, real-life and real-time experiences, and the extensive use of semantic web technologies such as Semantic Tags and Semantic Robots for haptic engagement and discovery learning.

The Impact of COVID-19

The global COVID-19 pandemic has dramatically transformed the delivery of education, highlighting the role of technology as a key enabler in extending the reach of the digital classroom. Despite its challenges, the pandemic has accelerated the shift towards online learning, breaking down temporal, spatial, and financial barriers.

Edtech has moved classrooms online, leveraging technology to create shared learning experiences and materials.

Learning is no longer confined to textbooks and physical classrooms. The use of interactive tools, videos, quizzes, e-books, and other digital resources provides students with real-time, real-life experiences. Technologies such as virtual reality (VR), augmented reality (AR), 3D simulations, Digital Twins, and 3D modeling have become integral to modern education, enabling continuous learning through both synchronous and asynchronous modes.

The Future of Digital Education

As we look to the future, the digital classroom will continue to evolve, integrating advanced technologies to enhance the learning experience. The ongoing adoption of TEL will drive improvements in education, preparing students for a rapidly changing world. By embracing these technological advancements, educators can provide personalized, engaging, and effective learning experiences that meet the diverse needs of all students.

The journey towards fully realizing the potential of digital education is ongoing, but the strides made thus far are promising. With continued innovation and strategic implementation, the future of education is bright, promising more accessible, inclusive, and effective learning for everyone.